Italian in a Week!

The Ultimate Italian Learning Course for Beginners

© **Copyright 2016 - All rights reserved.**

This document is geared towards providing exact and reliable information in regards to the topic and issue covered. The publication is sold with the idea that the publisher is not required to render accounting, officially permitted, or otherwise, qualified services. If advice is necessary, legal or professional, a practiced individual in the profession should be ordered.

- From a Declaration of Principles which was accepted and approved equally by a Committee of the American Bar Association and a Committee of Publishers and Associations.

In no way is it legal to reproduce, duplicate, or transmit any part of this document in either electronic means or in printed format. Recording of this publication is strictly prohibited and any storage of this document is not allowed unless with written permission from the publisher. All rights reserved.

The information provided herein is stated to be truthful and consistent, in that any liability, in terms of inattention or otherwise, by any usage or abuse of any policies, processes, or directions contained within is the solitary and utter responsibility of the recipient reader. Under no circumstances will any legal responsibility or blame be held against the publisher for any reparation, damages, or monetary loss due to the information herein, either directly or indirectly.

Respective authors own all copyrights not held by the publisher.

The information herein is offered for informational purposes solely, and is universal as so. The presentation of the information is without contract or any type of guarantee assurance.

The trademarks that are used are without any consent, and the publication of the trademark is without permission or backing by the trademark owner. All trademarks and brands within this book are for clarifying purposes only and are the owned by the owners themselves, not affiliated with this document.

Table of Contents

Introduction 1
Chapter 1 – The Italian Alphabet and Numbers 2
    The Italian Alphabet 2
    Counting the Italian Way 4
Chapter 2 - ALL ABOUT PRONUNCIATION 7
    Pronouncing Italian Vowels 7
    Dipthongs and Tripthongs 11
    Pronouncing Consonants 14
    Double Consonants and Consonantic Digraphs 20
    How to Stress Italian Words Properly 24
Chapter 3 - WELCOME TO ITALY 30
    Greetings! 30
    Describing Yourself 30
    Talk about Your Interests 36
Chapter 4 - A MATTER OF TIME4 39
    Telling the Time 39
    How to Set Up a Meeting in Italian? 43
    Days, Months, Year and Seasons 44
    Let's Talk about the Weather 47
Chapter 5 - DISTANCE, WEIGHT & DIRECTIONS 50

- Distance and Weight 50
- Asking for Directions 52

Chapter 6 - ITALIAN NOUNS 57
- Rules of Regular Nouns 58
- Rules of Irregular Nouns 61
- Nouns with Double Gender 64
- Articles 65

Chapter 7 – ADJECTIVES 71
- Rules of Adjectives 71
- Placement of Italian Adjectives 74
- Talk about Italian Colors 75
- Describe Your Feelings 76

Chapter 8 - PRONOUNS & VERBS 78
- Pronouns 78
- Verbs 80
- ESSERE (to be) 86
- AVERE (to have) 86

Chapter 9 - TRAVEL VOCABULARY 88
- Finding Accommodation 88
- Food 91

Conclusion 94

Introduction

I want to thank you and congratulate you for purchasing this book...

"Italian Basics in a Week!"

ITALIA! It is the best reason to make the effort to learn a new language.

Italy is one of the most beautiful countries in the world. The sights are breathtaking. The language is romantic. And it is historically rich. Italy is a splendid place to be for tourists. Lovely and luscious, Italia does not only offer exquisite cuisine and amazing historical sites, fantastic landscapes and jaw dropping fashion. Italia is not only a destination. It is a total experience.

Italia experience is far more beautiful and enjoyable if you know the language or at least the essentials. And that is exactly what's this book is for. So are you ready for the lesson of a lifetime? Get on with it and start speaking one of the most romantic languages in the world!

Thanks again for purchasing this book, I hope you enjoy it!

Chapter 1 – THE ITALIAN ALPHABET & NUMBERS

Learning a new language may seem too complex. But you have to remind yourself that learning something new whether it is a foreign language or a new skill can be overwhelming at first. If we break it down to simpler steps, however, we will eventually realize that it is doable.

Do you remember the first things you were taught in school? You may have forgotten most of the things you've learned back then but you will never forget the alphabet. That's where we start.

The Italian Alphabet

There are 21 letters in the Italian alphabet plus 5 letters of foreign origin. Here are the letters with their name and pronunciation.

A	*a*	pronounced as	AH
B	*bi*	pronounced as	BEE
C	*ci*	pronounced as	CHEE
D	*di*	pronounced as	DEE
E	*e*	pronounced as	AY
F	*effe*	pronounced as	EF-FAY
G	*gi*	pronounced as	JEE

H	*acca*	pronounced as	AHK-KA
I	*i*	pronounced as	EE
L	*elle*	pronounced as	EL-LAY
M	*emme*	pronounced as	EM-MAY
N	*enne*	pronounced as	EN-NAY
O	*o*	pronounced as	OH
P	*pi*	pronounced as	PEE
Q	*cu*	pronounced as	COO
R	*erre*	pronounced as	AIR-RAY
S	*esse*	pronounced as	ES-SAY
T	*ti*	pronounced as	TEE
U	*u*	pronounced as	OO
V	*vu* (or *vi*)	pronounced as	VOO (or VEE)
Z	*zeta*	pronounced as	ZAY-TAH

Letters of Foreign Origin

J	*i lunga*	pronounced as	EE LOON-GA
K	*cappa*	pronounced as	KAH-PAH
W	*doppia vu*	pronounced as	DOPE-PEE-AH VOO
X	*ics*	pronounced as	EEX
Y	*ipsilon*	pronounced as	EEP-SEE-LONE
	i greca	pronounced as	EE GRAY-KAH

Counting the Italian Way

We'll get into pronunciation lessons later. For now, let's learn another essential. Let's learn how to count the Italian way!

zero	0	{DSEH-roh}
uno	1	{OO-noh}
due	2	{DOO-way}
tre	3	{tray}
quattro	4	{KWAT-troh}
cinque	5	{CHEENG-kway}
sei	6	{SEH-yee}
sette	7	{SEHT-tay}
otto	8	{OT-toh}
nove	9	{NO-vay}
dieci	10	{DYEH-chee}
undici	11	{oon-DEE-chee}
dodici	12	{doh-DEE-chee}
tredici	13	{tray-DEE-chee}
quattordici	14	{kwaht-tohr-DEE-chee}
quindici	15	{kween-DEE-chee}
sedici	16	{say-DEE-chee}

diciassette	17	{dee-chah-SEHT-tay}
diciotto	18	{dee-CHOt-tO}
diciannove	19	{dee-chahn-NO-vay}
venti	20	{VEHN-tee}
ventuno	21	{vayn-too-noh}
ventidue	22	{vayn-tee-doo-way}
ventitré	23	{vayn-tee-tray}
ventiquattro	24	{vayn-tee-KWAHT-trO}
venticinque	25	{vayn-tee-CHEENG-kway}
trenta	30	{TRAYN-ta}
trentuno	31	{trayn-TOO-noh}
quaranta	40	{kwah-RAHN-tah}
cinquanta	50	{cheeng-KWAHN-tah}
sessanta	60	{says-SAHN-tah}
settanta	70	{sayt-TAHN-tah}
ottanta	80	{oht-TAHN-tah}
novanta	90	{noh-VAHN-tah}
cento	100	{CHEHN-toh}
centouno	101	{chayn-toh-oo-noh}

duecento	200	{dway-CHEHN-toh}
trecento	300	{tray-CHEHN-toh}
quattrocento	400	{kwaht-tro-CHEHN-toh}
cinquecento	500	{cheeng-kway-CHEHN-toh}
seicento	600	{say-CHEHN-toh}
settecento	700	{sayt-tay-CHEHN-toh}
ottocento	800	{ot-to-CHEHN-toh}
novecento	900	{no-vay-CHEHN-toh}
mille	1000	{MEEL-lay}

Chapter 2 - ALL ABOUT PRONUNCIATION

Pronouncing Italian Vowels

Italian vowel sounds vary. While the letter **A** only carries one sound, vowels **E** and **O** can have either open or closed sounds. Open vowel sounds are typically used in stressed syllabus. You will learn more about this later.

In Italian, the second to the last syllable or the penultimate carries the stress which is indicated by the grave accent (`` ` ``) placed over the letter **E**. This accent is also used over the vowels **A**, **O** and **U** if they are the last letters in a word. Closed sound on the other hand, is indicated by the acute accent (') over the letter **E**.

Pronunciation of closed and open sounds varies depending on the region. Another important thing to remember when pronouncing Italian vowels is that the letters I and U can have semi-vocal and vocal values. There are instances when the vowel **I** is silent specifically when it is followed by **C**, **G** or **SC**.

<u>Italian Vowel A</u>

Unlike in English or other languages where the pronunciation of **A** is often exaggerated or lengthened, Italian A is pronounced with a short and crisp "AH." Pronounce the following Italian words like the **A** in the English word "ask."

sala	which means	hall
fama	which means	fame
antipasto	which means	appetizer
amore	which means	love

Italian Vowel E

Like we said previously, the letter **E** has two pronunciations. It can have either an open or closed sound. How do they differ?

>**Open E** [ɛ] sound is a short EH, pronounced just like the letter E in the English word "met." Practice the open E sound with the following Italian words.

festa	which means	party or holiday
presto	which means	soon
testa	which means	head

>**Closed E** [e] sound is pronounced like a long AY like how you would pronounce the English word "they" except that there is no gliding I sound in the end. Try practicing the closed and open E sounds with the following Italian words. Remember, the open sound is usually applied in the stressed syllable (the penultimate) although the grave accent may not always be written.

mela	which means	apple
bene	which means	well
fede	which means	faith
bere	which means	to drink

Italian Vowel I

The pronunciation of this vowel depends on how it is used in a word. There are 3 possible pronunciations.

>**I** as EE like in "meet." Here are a few Italian words to practice on.

bimbo	which means	child
libro	which means	book
pino	which means	pine
vino	which means	wine

>**I** as a semivowel [j] pronounced like the Y in "yet."

chiamare {kYah-mah-ray}	which means	to call
fiume {fYu-may}	which means	river
piuma {pYu-mah}	which means	feather

>The Silent **I**

In the combinations, **sci**, **gi** and **ci** followed by **a**, **o**, **u**, the vowel **I** is not pronounced except when it has an accent over it. If there is an accent over I, ci is pronounced with a [ch] sound, gi is pronounced with a [j] sound and sci is pronounced with an [sh] sound.

In the following examples, I is silent.

arancia	which means	orange
giornale	which means	newspaper
giusto	which means	right or just
lasciare	which means	to leave
Scienza	which means	science

In the examples below, **I** carries the stress as it is in the second to the last syllable. In this case, it is pronounced with an [ee] sound.

bugia	which means	lie
analogia	which means	analogy
ecologia	which means	ecology

Italian Vowel O

Like E, the vowel **O** has two possible pronunciations. It is either open or closed.

>**Open O** is pronounced like in "or." This pronunciation is typically used in stressed syllables.

moda	which means	fashion
posta	which means	mail
toga	which means	toga

>**Closed O** is pronounced like in "oh," the same vowel sound used in the English word "awe."

nome	which means	name

Now, try pronouncing these words.

dono	which means	gift
mondo	which means	world

tavolo   which means   table

Italian Vowel U

This vowel is usually pronounced with an [oo] sound like in "boot."

fungo   which means   mushroom

luna   which means   moon

lungo   which means   long

tubo   which means   tube

There are exceptions however. If the letter **U** appears right before a vowel, it should be pronounced with a semivowel [w]. Here are a few examples.

guardare   which means   guard

guerra   which means   war

Dipthongs

Two vowels may be combined. In this case, they would make one sound.

>**ai** makes an AHY sound like in "sigh"

bailare   which means   to dance

>**au** makes an AHW sound like in "cow"

automobile   which means   car

>**ei** makes an EHY sound like in "say"

sei   which means   six

>**oi** makes an OY sound like in "joy"

poi   which means   later or then

>**ia** makes a YAH sound

bianco   which means   white

>**ie** makes a YEH or YAY sound

lieto   which means   happy

>**io** makes a YOH sound like in "yogurt"

fiore   which menas   flower

>**iu** makes a WEE sound

suino   which means   pig

>**uo** makes a WOH sound

nuovo   which means   new

Practice dipthong pronunciation with the following Italian words.

buono   which means   good

chiuso   which means   closed

ieri   which means   yesterday

invidia   which means   envy

più   which means   more

Tripthongs

Three vowels may also be combined resulting to a single sound. The usual combination consists of the unstressed I and a dipthong. Here are a few examples of tripthongs.

buoi {bWOY}   which means   oxen

miei {mYEY}   which means   mine

suoi {sWOY}   which means   his

tuoi {tWOY}   which means   yours

A dipthong and another vowel may be combined although they may not necessarily be considered as a tripthong. Here are a few examples.

baia {bAH-Yah}   which means   bay

febbraio {fEH-brah-YO}   which means   February

fioraio {fYO-rah-YOh}   which means   florist

noia {nO-Yah}   which means   boredom

Two dipthongs may also be combined to form one sound like in the following examples.

acquaio {ahk-KWah-Yoh}   which means   sink

ghiaia {gYAH-Yah}   which means   gravel

gioiello {JOH-Yeh-loh}   which means   jewel

muoio {mWO-Yo}   which means   die

Pronouncing Consonants

Italian consonants **B**, **F**, **M** and **V** sound similar to their English counterparts. Other consonants however, sound differently. Their pronunciation varies according to how they are used.

Italian C

[K] sound for a C that appears before **a**, **o**, **u** or another consonant. Take a look at the following examples.

cane {Kah-nay}   which means   dog

con {Kohn}   which means   with

culla {Kool-lah}   which means   cradle

credere {Kray-deh-ray}   which means   believe or think

[CH] sound for a C that appears before **i** or **e** like in "CHest."

aceto {ah-CHeh-toh}	which means	vinegar
cena {CHay-nah}	which means	supper
cibo {CHee-boh}	which means	food
cipolla {CHEE-po-llah}	which means	onion

Italian D

Just like its English counterpart, Italian D carries a **[d] sound**. The difference is that the Italian D is more explosive. To get the pronunciation right, you must position your tongue near the edge of the upper teeth without any aspiration. Let's try pronouncing these words.

data {Dah-tah}	which means	date
denaro {Day-nah-roh}	which means	money
donna {Do-nnah}	which means	woman
dove {Do-vay}	which means	where

Italian G

[G] sound like in English if the consonant appears before **a, o, u** or another consonant.

gamba {Gah-mbah}	which means	leg
gomma {Go-mmah}	which means	eraser
gusto {Goo-stoh}	which means	taste

grande {Grah-nday}   which means   great

[J] sound if it is placed before **i** or **e**.

gelato {Jeh-lah-toh}   which means   ice cream

gente {Jeh-ntay}   which means   people

gita {Jee-tah} which   which means   tour

pagina {pah-Jee-nah}   which means   page

Italian H is always silent.

ho {oh}   which means   have (I)

hai {ahy}   which means   have (you)

ha {ah}   which means   has (he/she/it)

hanno {ah-nnoh}   which means   have (they)

ahi! {ah-ee}   which means   ouch!

hotel {o-tehl}   which means   hotel

Italian L

It sounds similar to its English counterpart except that the former is sharper. Note the **L** in the English word "link."

lingua {Llee-ngwah}   which means   language

luna {Lloo-nah}   which means   moon

lungo {Lloo-ngoh}   which means   long

olio {o-Llyoh}   which means   oil

Italian N

This consonant is usually pronounced just like its English counterpart but it may also carry different sounds depending on the situation.

[NG] sound for an N before or after **C** or **G**

un cavallo {ooNG-kah-vah-Lloh}   which means a horse

campagna {kahm-pah-NGNYah}   which means field

banco {bah-ngkoh}   which means desk

Congresso {kohng-greh-soh}   which means congress

[M] sound if it appears before **P** or **B**

un bambino {am bam-bee-no}   which means   a child

un po {am po}   which means   some quantity of...

Nasalized [M] sound if it appears before **F** or **V**

un vento	which means	a wind
un frate	which means	a friar
inverno	which means	winter
infrastruttura	which means	infrastructure

Italian P

It carries the same sound just like its English counterpart except that the Italian P is pronounced without any aspiration sound.

pane {Pah-nay}	which means	bread
pasto {Pah-stoh}	which means	meal
pepe {Peh-Pay}	which means	pepper
ponte {Po-ntay}	which means	bridge

Italian Q

[KW] sound if it is found before **U** just like in the "quest"

quadro {KWah-droh}	which means	picture
quale {KWah-lay}	which means	which
quanto {kWah-ntoh}	which means	how much
questo {KWeh-stoh}	which means	this

Italian R

It has a **trilled sound**. To pronounce the Italian R correctly, flip your tongue and let it brush against the gums of the upper teeth. Practice with the following words.

albergo {ahl-behR-goh}	which means	hotel
arte {ahR-tay}	which means	art
ora {oh-Rah}	which means	now

orologio {oh-Roh-lo-joh} which means watch

Italian S

[Z] sound if it is placed in between **2 vowels** or before **B, D, G, L, M, N, R** and **V**.

casa {kah-Zah}	which means	house
sbaglio {Zbahg-lyoh}	which means	mistake
sgridare {Zgree-dah-ray}	which means	to scold
svelte {Zvehl-toh}	which means	quick

[S] sound elsewhere

pasare {pah-Sah-ray}	which means	to pass
soggiorno {Soh-jor-noh}	which means	living room
stanza {Stah-ntsa}	which means	room
stufato {Stoo-fah-toh}	which means	stew

Italian T

It has a **[T] sound** just like its English counterpart except that it is pronounced without any aspiration sound.

antipasto {ahn-Tee-pah-sToh}	which means	appetizer
carta {kahr-Tah}	which means	paper
matita {mah-Tee-Tah}	which means	pencil

testa {TEH-stah}   which means   head

Italian Z

Voiceless [TS] sound in these Italian words

Dizionario {dee-TSyoh-nah-ryoh}   which means   dictionary
grazie {grah-TSyay}   which means   thank you
negozio {nay-go-TSyoh}   which means   store
pizza {pee-TSah}   which means   pizza

Voiced [DS] sound just like in "beds."

pranzo {prahn-DSoh}   which means   lunch
romanzo {roh-mahn-DSoh}   which means   novel
zanzara {DSahn-DSah-rah}   which means   mosquito
zebra {DSeh-brah}   which means   zebra

Double Consonants

All Italian consonants can be doubled except for H and Q.

The sound for double F, L, M, N, R, S and V must be prolonged.

The stop sound for double B, C, D, G, P and T on the other hand, is stronger.

While double Z is pronounced the same as a single Z, double S sound is unvoiced.

Practice double consonants pronunciation with the following Italian words.

albicocca {ahl-bee-koK-Kah}   which means apricot

anno { ahN-Noh}   which means year

babbo {bahB-Boh}   which means dad

basso {bahS-Soh}   which means short

pennello {payn-nehL-Loh}   which means paint brush

ferro {fehR-Roh}   which means iron

fetta {fayT-Tah}   which means slice

evviva {ayV-Vee-vah}   which means hurrah

espresso {ays-prehS-Soh}   which means espresso coffee

cavalletto {kah-vahL-LayT-Toh}   which means easel

bistecca {bees-tayK-Kah}   which means beef steak

bello {behL-Loh}   which means beautiful

mamma {mahM-Mah}   which means mama

ragazzo {rah-gahT-TSO}   which means boy

spaghetti {Spah-ghayT-Tee}   which means spaghetti

tavolozza {tah-voh-loT-TSah} which means palette

Consonantic Digraphs

GH has a **[G] sound** like in "get"

ghetto {Gayt-Toh}   which means   ghetto
laghi {lah-Gee}   which means   lakes
maghi {mah-Gee}   which means   magicians

GLI is pronounced like the letter L in "million"

aglio {ah-LYoh}   which means   garlic
bottiglia {boht-tee-LYah}   which means   bottle
famiglia {fah-mee-LYah}   which means   family
meglio {mehL-LYoh}   which means   better

GN has an **[NY] sound** like in "canyon"

bagno {bah-NYO}   which means   bath

signora {see-NYo-rah}   which means   lady

signore {see-NYo-ray}   which means   gentleman

signorina {see-NYoh-ree-nah} which means   young lady

CH carries a **[K] sound**.

anche {ahng-Kay}   which means   also

che {Kay}   which means   that

chi {Kee}   which means   who

perché {payr-Kay}   which means   because

SC may be pronounced in two ways.

[SK] sound if it is followed by A, O or U

scarpa {SKahr-pah}   which means   shoe

scaloppina {SKah-lohp-pee-nah} which means   cutlets

pesca {pay-SKah}   which means   peach

ascoltare {ah-SKOl-tah-ray}   which means   to listen

[SH] sound if it is followed by I or E

scena {SHeh-nah}   which means   scene

pesce {pay-SHay}   which means   fish

crescere {Kray-SHay-ray}   which means   to grow

conoscere {koh-noh-SHay-ray}   which means   to know

SCH sounds like **[sk]**. It is usually found before E or I.

dischi {dee-SKee}   which means   records or disks

tasche {tah-SKay}   which means   pockets

lische {lee-SKay}   which means   fishbones

fiaschi {fee-yah-SKee}   which means   flasks

How to Stress Italian Words Properly

We've mentioned stress and accents before. In Italian, the penultimate or second to the last syllable is usually stressed. As with any other rule, there are always a few exceptions.

The **acute** (´) and **grave** (`) accents indicates stress on the syllable. The grave accent is typically used on vowels A, E, I, O and U. The acute accent on the other hand, may only be used on E and O. This accent indicates an open sound on E and O. Hence, è carries an [EH] sound and ò carries an [O] sound.

<u>Stress on Penultimate Syllables</u>

Below, you will find a list of Italian words that are stressed on the second to the last syllable. Remember your lessons on pronunciation and do not forget to stress the syllables properly.

uomo	{ WO-moh }	which means man
telefonare	{tay-lay-fo-NAH-ray}	which means telephone
studiare	{stu-DYAH-ray}	which means to study
signorina	{see-nyoh-REE-nah}	which means Miss
parlare	{pahr-LAH-ray}	which means to speak
padre	{PAH-dray}	which means father
nipote	{nee-POH-tay}	which means nephew
Milano	{mee-LAH-no}	which means Milan
foglia	{FOH-lyah}	which means leaf
amico	{ah-MEE-ko}	which means friend

There are Italian words that end in e but the final letter is dropped when they are followed by proper names. They serve as masculine titles. Even if the final e is dropped, the stress position is not affected. Here are a few examples.

dottore	{ dot-TO-ray }	which means doctor
dottor Nardi	{ dot-TOR Nardi }	which means Doctor Nardi
professore	{pro-fay-SOH-ray}	which means professor
professor Pace	{pro-fay-SOHR Pace}	which means professor Pace

Open O (ò) and E (è) may only be used on stressed syllables like in these Italian words.

telefono {te-LEH-foh-noh} which means telephone

nobile {NO-bee-lay} which means noble

medico {MEH-dee-koh} which means physician

automobile {ahw-toh-MO-bee-lay} which means automobile

If the stress lies on the penultimate syllable, you won't normally see an accent to indicate it. If however, the stress should be on the last vowel, it is indicated by an accent placed over the last vowel such as in the following words.

virtù {veer-TOO} which means virtue

venerdì {vay-nayr-DEE} which means Friday

università {oo-nee-vayr-see-TAH} which means university

tassì {tahs-SEE} which means taxi

però {pay-RO} which means however

perchè {payr-KEH} which means because

città {cheet-TAH} which means city

cioè {chow-EH} which means namely

An accent placed over the last letter of the word is sometimes essential especially when there is a need to emphasize a point being made. Such accents may be used on nouns, adverbs, verb inflections, etc.

perciò   {payr-CHO}   which means   therefore

però   {pay-RO}   which means   but/ however

farò   {fah-RO}   which means   I'll do...

più   {PYOO}   which means   plus/ more

Italian words with a –che ending are spelled out using an accent over the final e. With an accent over e, -che adopts a [KAY] sound.

perché   {payr-KAY}   which means   why or because

poiché   {pohy-KAY}   which means   because

benché   {bayng-KAY} which means   despite

giacché   {jahk-KAY}   which means   since

sicché   {seek-KAY}   which means   so or therefore

There are Italian words that are spelled exactly the same but mean different things depending in the stress position. Here are a few examples.

dà   {DAH}   meaning   gives

da	{DAH}	meaning	from
è	{AY}	meaning	is
e	{EH}	meaning	and
là	{LAH}	meaning	there
la	{LAH}	meaning	the/ it/ her
né	{NEH}	meaning	nor
ne	{NAY}	meaning	some
sé	{SHE}	meaning	himself/ herself
se	{SAY}	meaning	if
sì	{SEE}	meaning	yes
si	{SEE}	meaning	oneself
làvati	{LAH-vah-tee}	meaning	wash yourself
lavàti	{lah-VAH-tee}		masculine plural of washed

capitàno	{kah-pee-TAH-noh}	meaning	captain (noun)
càpitano	{KAH-pee-tah-noh}	meaning	they occur/ happen
règia	{REH-jah}	meaning	royal (adj.)
regìa	{ray-JYAH}	meaning	direction of play/movie
àncora	{AHN-koh-rah}	meaning	anchor (noun)
ancòra	{ahn-KO-rah}	meaning	again / more (adv)

REMINDER: Take note how the Italians put stress in their words. Understand the context of their statements. Read more Italian materials and continue to practice.

Chapter 3 –WELCOME TO ITALY

Greetings!

Now that you have learned basic pronunciation, let's try a few Italian words you can use every day to greet people and introduce yourself.

Benvenuto!	Welcome!
Ciao!	Hi!
Salute!	Cheers!
Buon giorno!	Good morning!
Buona sera!	Good evening!
Buona note.	Good night.

Describing Yourself

The Italians have two ways of speaking. They either use a formal tone or an informal one. While the formal tone is used for people with authority, the elderly or strangers, the informal tone is used for people you are more familiar with.

Come si chiama?	(formal)	
Come ti chiami?	(informal)	What is your name?
Mi chiamo _____ .		My name is _____ .

Da dove viene?	(formal)	Where are you from?
Da dove vieni?	(informal)	
Vengo da _____.		I am from _____.

Di che nazionalità è?	(formal)	What is your nationality?
Di che nazionalità sei?	(informal)	
(Io) sono _____.		I am _____.

Quanti anni ha?	(formal)	How old are you?
Quanti anni hai?	(informal)	
Ho [age] anni.		I am _____ years old.

Quando è nato/a?	(formal)	What is your birth date?
Quando sei nato/a?	(informal)	
Il mio compleanno è il DD/M/YYYY.		
My birthday is on DD/M/YYYY.		

È sposato/a?	(formal)	Are you married?
Sei sposato/a?	(informal)	
Sì, sono sposato/a.		Yes, I'm married.

No, non sono sposato/a.   No, I am not married.

Ha bambini?	(formal)	Do you have children?
Hai bambini?	(informal)	
Ha figli?	(formal)	
Hai figli?	(informal)	
Quanti figli ha?	(formal)	

How many children do you have?

Quanti figli hai?   (informal)

Sì, ho _____ bambini.	Yes, I have _____ children.
Sì, ho _____ figli.	Yes, I have _____ children.

Other keywords you may want to take note of include the following. They are not only important in conversations but also in filling up documents.

Nome	meaning	name
Nazionalità	meaning	nationality
Sesso	meaning	gender
Età	meaning	age
Data di nascita	meaning	date of birth
Indirizzo	meaning	address
Numero di telefono	meaning	telephone number

Numero di cellulare	meaning	cell phone number
Numero di passaporto	meaning	passport number

Piacere.	Nice to meet you.
Piacere di conoscerla.	Pleased to meet you
Parla l'inglese?	Do you speak English?
Si	Yes
No	No
Capisco	I understand
Non capisco	I do not understand
Mi scusi	Excuse me
Ripeta, per favore	Please repeat
Mi dispiace	I'm sorry
Per favore	Please
Grazie	Thank you
Prego	You're welcome
A dopo	See you later
Arrivederci	Goodbye

May I introduce my wife?

Permette che mi presnti mia moglie?

May I introduce my fiancé?

Permette che mi presenti mio fidanzato/a?

This is my friend, _____.

Le/ti presento un amico mi, _____.

How do you say _____ in Italian?

Come si dice _____ in italiano?

To help you out with country names, here is a list you can refer to.

L'Irlanda	for	Ireland
Il Galles	for	Wales
Il Giappone	for	Japan
L'Inghilterra	for	England
Gli Stati Uniti d'America	for	United States of America
La Germania	for	Germany
La Francia	for	France
La Spagna	for	Spain
La Colombia	for	Colombia
La China	for	China

Il Cile	for	Chile
Il Canada	for	Canada
La Scozia	for	Scotland
L'Australia	for	Australia
L'Argentina	for	Argentina

And here is a list of nationalities and their equivalent in the Italian language.

Scozzese	refers to	Scottish
Irlandese	refers to	Irish
Gallese	refers to	Welsh
Giapponese	refers to	Japanese
Inglese	refers to	English
Americano / Americana	refers to	American
Tedesco / Tedesca	refers to	German
Francese	refers to	French
Portoghese	refers to	Portuguese
Colombiano / Colombiana	refers to	Colombian
Cinese	refers to	Chinese

Cileno / Cilena	refers to	Chilean
Canadese	refers to	Canadian
Australiano / Australiana	refers to	Australian
Brasiliano / Brasiliana	refers to	Brazilian

Talk about Your Interests

What do you do in your free time?
Che cosa fai nel tempo libero?

What do you like doing best in your free time?
Che cosa ti piace fare di più il tempo libero?

To answer these questions, you can start by saying *Mi piace...* (I like...)

MI PIACE...

...*cantare*   meaning   ...singing

...*cucinare*	meaning	...cooking
...*leggere*	meaning	...reading
...*correre*	meaning	...running
...*nuotare*	meaning	...swimming
...*pescare*	meaning	...fishing
...*viaggiare*	meaning	...traveling
...*sciare*	meaning	...skiing
...*ballare*	meaning	...dancing
...*camminare*	meaning	...walking
...*rilassarmi*	meaning	...to relax
...*fare immersioni*	meaning	...scuba diving
...*andare in discoteca*	meaning	...night-clubbing
...*mangiare fuori*	meaning	...eating out
...*andare al cinema*	meaning	...going to the cinema
...*andare a teatro*	meaning	...going to the theatre
...*fare fotografie*	meaning	...taking photographs
...*incontrare amici*	meaning	...meeting friends
...*suonare musica*	meaning	...playing music

...*navigare in internet*	meaning	...surfing the internet
...*guardare films*	meaning	...watching movies
...*ascoltare musica*	meaning	...listening to music
...*giocare a pallacanestro*	meaning	...playing basketball
...*giocare a calcio*	meaning	...playing soccer

Here are some of the question words that can help you clarify things or seek further information.

Che cos'e?	What is that?
Chi e?	Who is it?
Dov'e _____?	Where is _____?
Quanto costa?	How much?
Perche?	Why?
Quando?	When?
Come?	How?

We will go back to more useful phrases after our lesson on Italian Numbers.

Chapter 4 – A MATTER OF TIME

You now know numbers. It's time to learn all about the Italian time.

Telling the Time

Che ore sono? –This is what you ask if you want to know the time.

The response usually starts with *Sono le...* followed by the hour and the minute.

Please note that the Italians use a 24-hour code.

So if it's 3:30pm, the response will be

Sono le quindici e trenta   OR   *Sono le quindici e mezzo*

*Note in the second statement that instead of saying the minutes in numbers (trenta), another word is used (e mezzo) which means "half past 3." There are other expressions which may be used. It will help if you familiarize yourself with all the possibilities.

e un quarto	and a quarter
meno dieci	ten minutes to
meno un quatro	a quarter to

Sono le cinque.	It's 5 a.m.

Sono le cinque e quindici.	It's 5:15 a.m.
Sono le cinque e un quarto.	It's 5:15 a.m.
É mezzanotte.	It's midnight.
É mezzogiorno.	It's noon.
É l'una.	It's 1 a.m.

General Terms Indicating Time of Day

The following are general terms which may also be used to indicate the time of day or answer the question WHEN?

giorno	meaning	day
oggi	meaning	today
mezzanotte	meaning	midnight
mezzogiorno	meaning	noon
di notte	meaning	in the dawn (midnight to around 5 a.m.)
di sera	meaning	in the evening
del pomeriggio	meaning	in the afternoon
allóra di pranzo	meaning	at lunchtime
prima di pranzo	meaning	before lunch
nella di mattina	meaning	in the morning
ora	meaning	now
subito	meaning	straight away

ieri	meaning	yesterday
domani	meaning	tomorrow
dopodomani	meaning	the day after tomorrow
tra tre giorno	meaning	in three days
presto/ tra poco	meaning	soon
più tardi	meaning	later
tardi	meaning	late
più presto	meaning	earlier
presto	meaning	early
in qualche momento	meaning	sometime (unspecified)
prima o poi	meaning	sometime/ eventually

QUANDO? ~ "WHEN?"

Let's go back to the question. There are other keywords that may be used along with this question word. If you are waiting for the plane or waiting on a bus, you may want to know when the plane arrives or what time the bus leaves. In the same manner, you may want to know when the shop closes or what time the movie starts. Here are the keywords to help you complete your sentences.

arriva	meaning	arrive
parte	meaning	leave

aperta	meaning	open
chiuso	meaning	close
comincia	meaning	start

Here are a few sample questions to help you complete your thoughts whatever kind of information you want to know.

When is the museum closed?
QUANDO è chiuso il museo?

When is the museum open?
QUANDO è aperta il museo?

When does the bus leave?
QUANDO parte l'autobus?

When does the train arrive?
QUANDO arriva il treno?

When does the game start?
QUANDO comincia la partita?

How to Set Up a Meeting in Italian?

Setting a meet with someone using the language is not that difficult. You can start with the following basic words and phrases.

Note that there are two ways to communicate in Italian. One is using the formal tone and the other using the casual tone.

Quando ci dobbiamo incontrare?

Quando ci vediamo?　　　When shall we meet?

Casual Tone

Quando ti va meglio?

Quando ti fa comodo?　　When is best for you?

Formal Tone

Quando Le fa comodo?　　When is the best time for you?

Here are a few options to watch out for or to ask yourself.

Questa settimana?	This week?
La prossima settimana?	Next week?
In quale giorno della settimana?	On which day of the week?
Durante il fine settimana?	During the weekend?
Per la fine della settimana?	By the end of the week?
All'inizio della settimana?	At the beginning of the week?

It's not only important to answer the question WHEN. Deciding on the meeting point is just as essential.

punto di incontro — meeting point

Dove ci dobbiamo incontrare? — Where shall we meet?

You can start your responses with:

Incontriamoci...

I'll meet you.../meet me...let's meet...

Incontriamoci per un drink dopo.

Let's meet up for a drink later.

Incontriamoci davanti all'hotel Woolrich intorno all'ora di cena.

Let's meet in front of the Woolrich hotel around dinner time.

Days, Months, Year and Seasons

Please note that the Italians do not use capital words for their days and months.

Italian DAYS

lunedì   {loo-nay-DEE}   Monday

martedì	{mahr-tay-DEE}	Tuesday
mercoledì	{mayr-koh-lay-DEE}	Wednesday
giovedì	{joh-vay-DEE}	Thursday
venerdì	{vay-nayr-DEE}	Friday
sabato	{sah-bah-toh}	Saturday
domenica	{doh-may-nee-KAH}	Sunday

Che giorno è oggi?	(What day is it?)
Oggi è sabato.	(Today is Saturday.)
Domani è domenica.	(Tomorrow is Sunday.)

Italian Months

Month in Italian is *i mesi*. The first letter of Italian months just like the days of the week is not capitalized.

gennaio	{ jayn-NAH-yoh}	January
febbraio	{fayb-BRAH-yoh}	February
marzo	{MAHR-tsoh}	March
aprile	{ah-PREE-lay}	April
maggio	{MAHJ-jyoh}	May
giugno	{JOO-nyoh}	June
luglio	{LOOL-lyoh}	July

agosto	{ah-GOS-toh}	August
settembre	{sayt-TEHM-bray}	September
ottobre	{oht-TOH-bray}	October
novembre	{noh-VEHM-bray}	November
dicembre	{dee-SEHM-bray}	December

Italian Year

Year in Italian is *anno*. It is read and spelled out differently.

In English for instance, 1982 is nineteen eighty two. The Italians use this format for their year: nineteen hundred eighty-two.

1982	is	*mille novecentottantadue.*
1883	is	*mille diciotto cento ottanta tre*
1961	is	*mille novecento sessanta uno*
1995	is	*mille novecento novanta cinque*
2008	is	*mille duecento otto*
2012	is	*mille duecento dodici*
2016	is	*mille duecento sedici*

Italian Seasons

Season in Italian is *le stagioni*.

la primavera	{lah pree-mah-VEH-rah}	Spring

l'estate	{lays-TAH-tay}	Summer
l'autunno	{lahw-TOON-noh}	Autumn
l'inverno	{leem-VEHR-noh}	Winter

Let's Talk about the Weather

Since we're on the topic of seasons, let's talk about the weather. One of the most excellent ways of breaking the ice is to talk about the weather. To make sure you have everything you need to engage in small talk, we have laid out here sample phrases and words to improve your vocabulary.

As usual, we begin with the questions.

Com'è il tempo?	meaning	How is the weather?
Che tempo fa?	meaning	What is the weather like?
Che tempo fa fuori?	meaning	What is it like outside?

Quali sono le previsioni del tempo per oggi/ questa settimana?

What is the weather forecast for today/ this week?

The following are some of the most generic responses you can give or get.

Il tempo è bello.	meaning	The weather is nice.
Fa bel tempo.	meaning	It is a good weather.
È bel tempo.	meaning	It is beautiful weather.
Fa cattivo tempo.	meaning	It is miserable weather.

Fa un tempo orribile.	meaning	It is terrible weather.
È brutto tempo.	meaning	It is bad weather.

There are however, more specific answers like the following.

Fa caldo.	meaning	The weather is hot.
È soleggiato.	meaning	It is sunny.
E' umido.	meaning	It is humid.
È ventoso.	meaning	It is windy.
Il cielo è sereno.	meaning	The sky is clear.
È nuvoloso.	meaning	It is cloudy.
Sta piovendo or piove.	meaning	It is raining.
È burrascoso.	meaning	It is stormy.

Fa freddo.	meaning	It is cold.
Sta nevicando or nevica.	meaning	It is snowing.
Fa un freddo gelido.	meaning	It's icy cold.

Feel free to use the following terms when you chat about the weather.

L'arcobaleno	meaning	the rainbow
La nuvola	meaning	the cloud
La grandine	meaning	the hail

Il fiocco di neve	meaning	the snowflake
La pioggia	meaning	the rain
La neve	meaning	the snow
Il tuono	meaning	the thunder
Il ghiaccio	meaning	the ice
Il temporale	meaning	the thunderstorm
L'inondazione	meaning	the flood
Il lampo	meaning	the lightning
La nebbia	meaning	the fog
Il terremoto	meaning	the earthquake
La temperatura	meaning	the temperature
La tempesta	meaning	the storm
L'uragano	meaning	the hurricane

Chapter 5 - DISTANCE, WEIGHT & DIRECTIONS

Whether you are buying goods or asking for directions, it is important that you familiarize yourself with these terms. It will be helpful when you are trying to get around Italy or shopping for some items too.

Distance and Weight

Note that the Italians use the metric system.

Distance

chilometro   {kee-loh-MEH-troh}   which means kilometer

metro   {MEH-troh}   which means meter

millimetro   {meel-lee-MEH-troh}   which means millimeter

centimetro   {chehn-tee-MEH-troh}   which means centimeter

If you want to inquire about the distance you have to travel to get to a certain place, you start the question with *QUANTA DISTA...* (How far...)

QUANTA DISTA...

la mostra d'arte?   (...is the art exhibition?)

la stazione ferroviara?   (...is the train station?)

una banca?   (...is the bank?)

un bagno pubblico? (...is the public restroom?)

l'ospedale? (...is the hospital?)

la fermata dell'autobus? (...is the bus stop?)

Weight

In Italian, weight is *peso*. If you're shopping for a food item, you may be asked this.

Quanto è necessario? How much do you need?

Take note of the following units of measurement in Italian.

milligrammo	meaning	milligram
grammo	meaning	gram
ettogrammo	meaning	hectogram
chilogrammo	meaning	kilogram
quinatle	meaning	quintal
tonnelatta	meaning	ton
millilito	meaning	milliliter
litro	meaning	liter
mezzo litro	meaning	half liter

Asking for Directions

Now that you understand distances, you've got the basics for understanding directions. Expand your vocabulary with these Italian words so you can ask and understand directions well.

You can get a map but it will be easier if you know the right questions to ask. You can use the following as guide.

Formal tone

Mi Scusi! Potrebbe dirmi dove si trova _____ per favore?

Excuse me please! Could you please tell me where _____ is?

Sa dove si trova _____?

Do you know where _____ is?

Casual tone

Scusa! Potresti dirmi dove si trova _____ per favore?

Excuse me please! Could you please tell me where _____ is?

Sai dove si trova _____?

Do you know where _____ is?

Come posso arrivare al _____ *?*

How do I get to _____?

Dove posso trovare _____ *per cortesia?*

Where can I find _____, please?

You can fill in the blanks with the following Italian terms for the places you will likely want to find.

La stazione dei treni	meaning	the train station
Il bar	meaning	the bar
Il monumento	meaning	the monument
La periferia	meaning	the suburb
Il centro città	meaning	the town center
Il municipio	meaning	the town hall
Il parco	meaning	the park
L'ospedale	meaning	the hospital
I bagni pubblici/ Le toilette pubbliche	meaning	the public restrooms
La stazione di polizia	meaning	the police station
Il centro storico	meaning	the historic center
Il centro commerciale	meaning	the shopping center

L'agenzia di viaggio	meaning	the travel agency
La strada	meaning	the street

Now that you know how to ask the questions, you also have to take note of the responses. Most likely, the responses will start with the following.

Formal

Prenda...	meaning	take...
Attraversa...	meaning	cross...
Segua...	meaning	follow...
Vada...	meaning	go...

Informal

Prendi...	meaning	take...
Attraversi...	meaning	cross...
Segui...	meaning	follow...
Vai...	meaning	go...

Here is a list of the terms you are likely to encounter.

A est	meaning	to the east
A sud	meaning	to the south

A nord	meaning	to the north
A ovest	meaning	to the west
All'inizio di	meaning	at the beginning of
Alla fine di	meaning	at the end of
Dritto / diritto	meaning	straight
A destra	meaning	to the right
A sinistra	meaning	to the left
Destra	meaning	right
Sinistra	meaning	left
Vicino a	meaning	next to
Di fronte a	meaning	in front of
Il ponte	meaning	the bridge
L'angolo	meaning	the corner
La prossima strada	meaning	the street after the next
Dietro l'angolo	meaning	around the corner
La prossima strada a destra	meaning	the next street to the right

If you're unsure about the distance, you can further clarify using the following as guide.

È vicino?	meaning	Is it close by?
È molto lontano?	meaning	Is it very far?

Non è vicino.	meaning	It is not close by.
È lontano.	meaning	It is far.
È vicino.	meaning	It is close by.
Non è lontano.	meaning	It is not far.

Chapter 6 –NOUNS & ARTICLES

Let's take a moment to discuss one of the most basic parts of speech. Throughout the previous lessons, you have encountered Italian nouns. This chapter is supposed to introduce you on how Italian nouns work.

There are basically two major types of nouns: common and proper. In Italian, common nouns are called *nomi comuni* and proper nouns are called *nomi propi*.

Nomi Comuni

cane	meaning	dog
ragazzo	meaning	kid
bellezza	meaning	beauty
fiume	meaning	river
giustizia	meaning	justice
speranza	meaning	hope

Nomi Propi

Roma	for	Rome
Italia	for	Italian

Rules of Regular Nouns

Most Italian nouns are governed by 3 basic rules and these are the following.

1. Masculine nouns with **-o** ending for singular form and **-i** ending in their plural form

2. Feminine nouns with **-a** ending for singular form and **-e** ending in their plural form

3. Nouns with **-e** ending for singular form and **-i** for plural form which can either be masculine or feminine

Masculine Nouns

Singular (-o ending)	Plural (-i ending)	English
tavolo	*tavoli*	table
museo	*musei*	museum
libro	*libri*	book
coro	*cori*	chorus
corpo	*corpi*	body
cielo	*cieli*	sky
appartamento	*appartamenti*	apartment
suono	*suoni*	sound

*So for regular masculine nouns, the rule is easy. They end with –o and if you want to use them in their plural form, all you need to do is change the ending from –o to –i and vice versa.

Feminine Nouns

Singular (-a ending)	Plural (-e ending)	English
cas*a*	cas*e*	house
finestr*a*	finestr*e*	window
sed*ia*	sed*ie*	chair
strad*a*	strad*e*	street
magliett*a*	magliett*e*	t-shirt
test*a*	test*e*	head
fotograf*ia*	fotograf*ie*	photo
penn*a*	penn*e*	pen

*Singular regular feminine nouns that end with –a can be turned into plural form by changing the ending to –e.

Masculine Nouns Ending in –e

Singular (-e ending)	Plural (-i ending)	English
bicchiere	*bicchieri*	glass
studente	*studenti*	student
ristorante	*ristoranti*	restaurant
fiume	*fiumi*	river
mese	*mesi*	month

Feminine Nouns Ending in -e

Singular (-e ending)	Plural (-i ending)	English
luce	*luci*	light
nube	*nubi*	cloud
ape	*api*	bee

*So how do you tell which nouns ending in –e or –i are feminine and which ones are masculine? The answer is simple. You memorize them. As you encounter them more often, you should be able to tell them apart much easier.

Rules of Irregular Nouns

Irregular nouns are much more challenging. And many Italian nouns fall into this category. Let's have a quick look at the rules that govern these nouns.

1. Some irregular nouns maintain their form whether they are singular or plural.

2. Singular masculine nouns with -ma ending adopt a -mi ending in their plural form.

3. Singular feminine nouns that end in -ga and -ca are turned into plural form by changing the ending to -ghe and -che respectively.

4. Singular masculine nouns that end with -co and -go may adopt a -chi and -ghi ending or -ci and -gi ending in their plural form.

Irregular Nouns that Maintain Their Form Whether They are Singular or Plural

There are sub-rules to take note of here. This category includes the following

>Feminine nouns with **-ie** ending

example: *speci<u>e</u>*   meaning   species

>Feminine nouns with **-o** ending

example: *aut<u>o</u>*   meaning   car

>Masculine neologism that end in **-o**

example: *euro*　　　　meaning　　　　Euro

>Nouns ending in **-i**

example: *analisi*　　　　meaning　　　　Analysis

>Nouns ending in an accented vowel

example: *università*　　　　meaning　　　　University

>Monosyllable nouns

example: *re*　　　　meaning　　　　King

>Foreign nouns

example: *goal, film*, etc.

Masculine Nouns (-ma and –mi ending)

Singular (-ma)	English	Plural (-mi)	English
tema	theme	*temi*	themes
problema	problem	*problemi*	problems

Feminine Nouns (-ca and –che ending)

Singular (-ca)	English	Plural (-che)	English
*domeni**ca***	Sunday	*domeni**che***	Sundays

Feminine Nouns (-ga and –ghe ending)

Singular (-ga)	English	Plural (-ghe)	English
*colle**ga***	Colleague	*colle**ghe***	colleagues

Singular Masculine Nouns (-co and –go ending)

Singular (-co, -go)	English	Plural	English
*tedes**co***	German	*tedes**chi***	Germans
*alber**go***	hotel	*alber**ghi***	hotels
*medi**co***	doctor	*medi**ci***	doctors
*psicolo**go***	psychologist	*psicolo**gi***	psychologists
*ami**co***	friend	*ami**ci***	friends
*dialo**go***	dialogue	*dialo**ghi***	dialogues

*Singular masculine nouns that end in –co and –go may adopt –chi and -ghi ending respectively IF the stress on the word is on the penultimate syllable.

**They adopt a –ci and –gi ending respectively IF the stress is on the third to the last syllable of the word.

So, irregular nouns are a tad bit more complex than the regular ones which follow simple rules. Don't worry! You don't have to memorize them all. Just take your time in reading and immersing yourself further into the language and take note of those you encounter.

Nouns with Double Gender

You've learned quite a bit about regular and irregular nouns along with the rules that govern them. Did you know that there is a third category? These are the nouns that seem to have a double gender. They seem to be flexible in that they can have a singular feminine and masculine form. These nouns share the same stem word. HOWEVER, when the ending is changed from –o to –a or vice versa, they may have a completely different meaning.

*tort**o***	versus	*tort**a***
(fault)		(cake)
*pian**to***	versus	*pian**ta***
(crying)		(plant)

*coll**o***　　versus　　*coll**a***

(neck)　　　　　　　　(glue)

*cors**o***　　versus　　*cors**a***

(avenue)　　　　　　　(running)

Articles

Articles are extremely important in the Italian language. In some cases, they may not be needed. But they are almost always used.

Definite Articles

In English, we have "the" as a definite article. It doesn't matter whether the noun is singular or plural, this article is still applicable. It's a different case for Italian however. Add to the fact that nouns are either masculine or feminine.

Definite Articles for Masculine Nouns

For singular masculine nouns, *il* and *lo* may be used. The definite article ***il*** is used when the noun starts with a consonant. ***Lo*** on the other hand, is used for nouns that start with s+consonant, z, ps, gn and y. If the noun begins with a vowel or h, ***l'*** is used. The plural form of the definite article il is ***i***. The plural equivalent of lo and l' is ***gli***. Let's map them out for a better view.

Singular	Plural
il pollo (the chicken) *il leto* (the bed)	*i polli* (the chickens) *i letti* (the beds)
lo student (the student) *lo zio* (the uncle) *lo yogurt* (the yogurt)	*gli student* (the students) *gli zii* (the uncles) *gli yogurt* (the yogurts)
l'ombrello (the umbrella) *l'antipasto* (the antipasto)	*gli ombrelli* (the umbrellas) *gli antipasti* (the antipastos)

Definite Articles for Feminine Nouns

Singular feminine nouns use **la** except when the first letter is a vowel or an h. In this case, la is contracted to **l'**. The plural form for both is **le**.

Singular	Plural
la porta (the door) *la zuppa* (the soup)	*la porte* (the doors) *la zuppe* (the soups)
l'amica (the friend) *l'ora* (the hour)	*le amiche* (the friends) *le ore* (the hours)

When to Use/Not Use Definite Articles

It was previously mentioned that articles are almost always used in Italian. Please take note of the following guide on when to use and when to avoid using definite articles.

USE: with titles like *signora, signore, signorina* and *dottore* when such titles appear before the surname.

il signor Bianchi

il dottor Vitale

la signora Rossi

DON'T USE: with titles like *signora, signore, signorina* and *dottore* for direct speech.

Dottor Vitale, come sta? Doctor Vitale, how are you?

USE: with name of countries, continents, isles and regions.

la Sicilia

la Toscana

l'Europa

DON'T USE: after the preposition *IN* with name of countries, continents, isles and regions.

in Sicilia

in Toscana

in Europa

USE: with sport and languages.

il tennis

l'Italiano

DON'T USE: after the verb *giocare a* with sport.

giocare a tennis

USE: with time.

Sono le due.　　　　It's 2:00 am.

USE: with material and colors.

il cotone

il rosso

DON'T USE: after preposition *DI* with materials

la camicia di cotone

Indefinite Articles

English definite articles are "a" and "an." While English has two, Italian has a total of four. The indefinite article used in the Italian language depends on the beginning letter of the noun and its gender.

Masculine nouns that begin with s, z, ps, gn and y, the indefinite article **uno** is used. For everything else, the indefinite article **un** is used. On the other hand, feminine nouns that begin with consonant use the indefinite article **una** while those that begin with vowels include **un'**. Let's have a closer look.

Masculine	Feminine
uno spumante (a sparkling) **uno** gnomo (a gnome)	**una** bottiglia (a bottle) **una** candela (a candle)
un appartamento (a flat) **un** momento (a moment)	**un'**aranciata (an orange juice) **un'**insalata (a salad)

Negative Indefinite Articles

As you have noticed these indefinite articles are reserved for singular nouns. They also have a negative counterpart. Instead of saying "a bottle", you can also say "bottle" using indefinite articles.

The negative equivalent of *uno* is **nessuno** and **nessun** for *un*. All feminine nouns take the negative indefinite article **nessuna**.

Masculine	Feminine
***nessuno** spumante* (no sparkling wine) ***nessuno** gnomo* (a gnome)	***nessuna** bottiglia* (a bottle) ***nessuna** candela* (a candle)
***nessun** appartamento* (a flat) ***nessun** momento* (a moment)	***nessuna** aranciata* (an orange juice) ***nessuna** insalata* (a salad)

Chapter 7 - ADJECTIVES

Adjectives are descriptive words. They may take an attributive or a predicative function like in the following examples.

Attributive function: *Il **luminoso** sole splende.* (The bright sun shines.)

Predicative function: *Il sole è **luminoso**.* (The sun is bright.)

In using Italian adjectives, there are plenty to consider. For one, the adjective in use must always agree with both the gender and number of the noun. In which case, a singular masculine noun calls for a singular masculine adjective and so on.

Rules of Adjectives

Earlier, you've learned about determining gender and number of nouns. We will now focus on adjectives. Take note of these rules governing Italian adjectives and be mindful in using them.

1. Singular masculine adjectives usually have an **-o** ending while singular feminine adjectives have an **-a** ending. You can convert a masculine adjective ending in -o to its feminine form by adopting an -a ending. Plural masculine adjectives ending in **-i** can be turned into feminine adjectives by changing the ending to **-e**.

Masculine	Feminine
Nuov**o**	nuov**a**
Nuov**i**	Nuov**e**

Take note of how articles, nouns and adjectives are used in the following examples.

le case nuove	meaning	the new houses
la casa nuova	meaning	the new house
i giochi nuovi	meaning	the new toys
il gioco nuovo	meaning	the new toy

2. If the adjective ends in -a, note whether or not it ends with **-ista**. In this case, the adjective is both masculine and feminine. Its plural masculine form should adopt an **-isti** ending and plural feminine form should have an **-iste** ending.

Masculine	Feminine
*Ego**ista***	*ego**ista***
*Ego**isti***	*Ego**iste***

le donne egoiste	meaning	the egoist women
gli uomini egoisti	meaning	the egoist men
la donna egoista	meaning	the egoist woman
l'uomo egoista	meaning	the egoist man

3. Some adjectives in their singular form for both masculine and feminine may end in **-e**. Their plural form takes **-i** ending. A good example of this is the Italian adjective *gentile* for kind. *Gentile* is singular and can be used for either masculine or feminine noun. The plural form is *gentili*.

le donne gentili	meaning	the kind women
gli uomini gentili	meaning	the kind men
la donna gentile	meaning	the kind woman
l'uomo gentile	meaning	the kind man

4. There are Italian adjectives with an invariable form. This group includes the following.

>*dispari* (odd) and *pari* (pair)

>adjectives referring to color whose names are derived from nouns: *rosa* (pink), *ocra* (ocher), *viola* (violet), *nocciola* (hazelnut), *marrone* (maroon)

>adjectives that are formed by combining the prefix **anti** with a noun: **anti**<u>furto</u> (anti-theft), **anti**<u>nebbia</u> (fog lights)

le case rosa	meaning	the pink houses
la casa rosa	meaning	the pink house
i muri rosa	meaning	the pink walls
il muro rosa	meaning	the pink wall

Placement of Italian Adjectives

Adjectives can either be placed after or before the noun they describe. The statement will still mean the same like in the following example.

Adjective before noun: *Si tratta di un **grande** lago*. (It is a big lake.)

Adjective after noun: *Si tratta di un lago **grande***. (It is a big lake.)

*You see, the statement still means the same thing. However, there are differences in the tone. In the Italian language, an adjective placed after a noun is more powerful than an adjective placed before the noun. In which case, if you want to emphasize the description, you are advised to place the adjective after the noun you wish to define.

In other words, an adjective before the noun can serve a descriptive function. On the other hand, an adjective after a noun can serve a distinctive function.

Adjective before noun:

*Il signore Vitale gode di una **bella** figlia.*

(Mr. Vitale has a beautiful daughter.)

Adjective after noun:

*Il signore Vitale gode di una figlia **bella**.*

(Mr. Vitale has a daughter, a beautiful one.)

HOWEVER, there is always an exception. In some cases, the position of the adjective can affect the meaning of the statement. Note the difference in these statements.

Adjective after noun:

*Il signore Vitale è un <u>uomo</u> **povero**.*

(Mr. Vitale is a poor man.)

Adjective before noun:

*Il signore Vitale è un **pover'**<u>uomo</u>.*

(Mr. Vitale is a mean man.)

Most adjectives can be placed either before or after the noun. However, there are some adjectives that SHOULD ONLY BE PLACED AFTER THE NOUN. This group includes the following.

>adjectives referring to nationality: *Americano, Tedesco, Italiano...*

>adjectives referring to membership: *comunista, socialista, democratico...*

>adjectives referring to location or position: *sinistro, destro...*

>adjectives referring to physical characteristics: *gobo, cieco...*

Talk about Italian Colors

arcobaleno	meaning	rainbow
multicolore	meaning	multi-colored

bronzo	meaning	bronze
argento	meaning	silver
oro	meaning	gold
grigio	meaning	gray
bianco	meaning	white
porpora / viola	meaning	purple
rosa	meaning	pink
marrone	meaning	brown
nero	meaning	black
verde	meaning	green
rosso	meaning	red
blu	meaning	blue
giallo	meaning	yellow
arancione	meaning	orange

Describe Your Feelings

You can start with *sono* (for I am...)

SONO...

...*di fretta*	meaning	...in a hurry
...*imbarazzato*	meaning	...embarrassed

...*triste*	meaning	...sad
...*tranquillo*	meaning	...calm
...*sorpreso*	meaning	...surprised
...*furioso*	meaning	...furious
...*preoccupato*	meaning	...worried
...*occupato*	meaning	...busy
...*nervoso*	meaning	...nervous
...*felice*	meaning	...happy
...*meravigliato*	meaning	...amazed
...*geloso*	meaning	...jealous
...*arrabbiato*	meaning	...angry
...*spaventato*	meaning	...frightened
...*agitato*	meaning	...excited
...*stanco*	meaning	...tired
...*annoio*	meaning	...bored
...*innamorato*	meaning	...in love

Chapter 8 – PRONOUNS & VERBS

You know about Italian nouns, articles and adjectives. It's time to get to know Italian pronouns and verbs. By the end of this lesson, you should be able to confidently formulate your own sentences.

Pronouns

These are what we use as substitute to nouns. They can be the subject of a sentence or sometimes, an object. We'll start with the most basic, personal subject pronouns.

<u>Subject Pronouns</u>

io	for	I
tu	for	You (singular)
lui	for	He
lei	for	She
noi	for	We
voi	for	You (plural)
loro	for	They

*These subject pronouns may be omitted from the sentence. The conjugation of the verb is enough to indicate the subject. You will learn about verb conjugation in the next lesson. For now, focus on the use of pronouns.

Direct Object Pronouns

Pronouns may also be the direct receiver of the action verb. For instance in English, you can say, "He loves me." In this case, "he" is the subject pronoun while "me" is the direct object pronoun. It gets a little more complex in Italian because the form of the direct object pronoun changes according to its placement in the sentence: whether it is positioned before or after the conjugated verb.

D.O. after verb	D.O. before verb	English	Example
me	*mi*	me	*Ama **me**.* (He loves me.) ***Mi** ama.*
te	*ti*	you (S)	*Ama **te**.* (He loves you.) ***Ti** ama.*
lui	*lo*	Him	*Amo **lui**.* (I love him.) ***Lo** amo.*
lei/Lei	*la/La*	Her	*Amo **lei**.* (I love her,) ***La** amo.*
noi	*ci*	Us	*Ama **noi**.* (He loves us.) ***Ci** ama.*
voi	*vi*	you (Pl)	*Amo **voi**.* (I love you.) ***Vi** amo.*
loro	*li*	them	*Ama **loro**.* (He loves them.) ***Li** ama.*

Indirect Object Pronoun

In contrast to definite pronouns that answer the questions "whom" or "what", indirect object pronouns answer the questions "to whom" or "for whom." In Italian, indirect object pronouns change in form according to their placement (before or after the conjugated verb).

I.O. after verb	I.O. before verb	English
a me	*mi*	(to/for) me
a te	*ti*	(to/for) you (S)
a lui	*gli*	(to/for) him
a lei/Lei	*la/La*	(to/for) her
a noi	*ci*	(to/for) us
a voi	*vi*	(to/for) you (Pl)
a loro	*gli*	(to/for) them

Verbs

The Italian language has two major types of verbs: regular and irregular. While regular verbs follow easier rules for conjugation, irregular verbs are more complex. For the interest of this lesson, we will stick to regular verbs for now in their present form.

Italian verbs can be grouped into three categories according to their endings.

>Verbs that end in –are

>Verbs that end in –ere

>Verbs that end in –ire

Regular Verbs Ending in -ARE

Here's how to conjugate verbs ending in –are. First, you must drop the ending and replace them with the following suffixes according to the subject. Let's use the verb *parl**are*** (to speak).

Subject	ENDING	Example
(Io)	-|o	Parl**o** ~ Parlo Italiano. (I speak Italian.)
(Tu)	-|i	Parl**i** ~ Parli Italiano. (You speak Italian.)
(lui/Lei)	-|a	Parl**a** ~ Parla Italiano. (He/She speaks Italian.)
(Noi)	-|iamo	Parl**iamo** ~ Parliamo Italiano. (We speak Italian.)
(Voi)	-|ate	Parl**ate** ~ Parlate Italiano. (You all speak Italian.)
(Loro)	-|ano	Parl**ano** ~ Parlano Italiano. (They speak Italian.)

Here are a few more regular Italian verbs ending in –ARE.

ascoltare	meaning	to listen
volare	meaning	to fly
abitare	meaning	to live

ballare	meaning	to dance
aspettare	meaning	to wait
lavorare	meaning	to work
cantare	meaning	to sing
ritornare	meaning	to return
girare	meaning	to turn
ispezionare	meaning	to inspect
arrivare	meaning	to arrive
domandare	meaning	to ask
cenare	meaning	to have dinner
camminare	meaning	to walk
dimenticare	meaning	to forget
ricordare	meaning	to remember
comprare	meaning	to buy
guardare	meaning	to watch
riposare	meaning	to rest

Regular Verbs -ERE

Follow the endings suggested below according to the subject to conjugate –ere verbs properly. For reference, we're using *VEDERE* (to see). Take note of how it is conjugated and used in sentences.

Subject	ENDING	Example
(Io)	-|o	*Ved**o** ~ Vedo te.* (I see you.)
(Tu)	-|i	*Ved**i** ~ Mi vedi.* (You see me.)
(lui/Lei)	-|e	*Ved**e** ~ Vede loro.* (He/She sees them.)
(Noi)	-|iamo	*Ved**iamo** ~ Vi vediamo.* (We see you all.)
(Voi)	-|ete	*Ved**ete** ~ Vedete lui.* (You all see him.)
(Loro)	-|ono	*Ved**ono** ~ Ci vedono.* (They see us.)

Here are a few more examples of regular verbs ending in -ere. You can practice conjugating them.

credere	meaning	to believe
vivere	meaning	to live
sorridere	meaning	to smile
ridere	meaning	to laugh
scrivere	meaning	to write
rispondere	meaning	to reply
piangere	meaning	to cry
perdere	meaning	to lose
leggere	meaning	to read
correre	meaning	to run
chiudere	meaning	to close

chiedere   meaning   to ask

accadere   meaning   to happen

Regular –IRE Verbs

There are two ways to conjugate regular verbs that end in –ire. To demonstrate this better, we're using two verbs: *SERVIRE* (to serve) and *CAPIRE* (to understand).

Subject	ENDING	SERVIRE (to serve)
(Io)	-|o	Serv**o**
(Tu)	-|i	Serv**i**
(lui/Lei)	-|e	Serv**e**
(Noi)	-|iamo	Serv**iamo**
(Voi)	-|ite	Serv**ite**
(Loro)	-|ono	Serv**ino**

Subject	ENDING	CAPIRE (to understand)
(Io)	isc + o	cap**isco**
(Tu)	isc + i	cap**isci**
(lui/Lei)	isc + e	cap**isce**
(Noi)	-|iamo	cap**iamo**
(Voi)	-|ite	cap**ite**
(Loro)	isc + ono	cap**iscono**

These regular -IRE verbs follow the *SERVIRE* conjugation.

sentire	meaning	to feel/hear
divertire	meaning	to enjoy
partire	meaning	to leave
mentire	meaning	to lie
aprire	meaning	to open
finire	meaning	to finish
riunire	meaning	to meet
impazzire	meaning	to go crazy
bollire	meaning	to boil
seguire	meaning	to follow
vestire	meaning	to dress
pulire	meaning	to clean

The following regular -IRE verbs follow the CAPIRE conjugation.

preferire	meaning	to prefer
gioire	meaning	to enjoy/ rejoice/ be delighted

*We leave out irregular verbs for now. However, it is important to get you acquainted with two important irregular verbs. These are ESSERE and AVERE.

ESSERE (to be)

You will notice here that irregular verbs do not exactly follow specific rules. You will need to familiarize yourself with this conjugation.

Subject	*ESSERE*	Examples
(Io)	**sono**	*Sono qui.* (I am here.)
(Tu)	**sei**	*Sei Italiano.* (You are Italian.)
(lui/Lei)	**è**	*È gentile.* (He/She is kind.)
(Noi)	**siamo**	*Siamo in vacanza.* (We are on vacation.)
(Voi)	**siete**	*Siete felice.* (You all are happy.)
(Loro)	**sono**	*Sono eccitati.* (They are excited.)

AVERE (to have)

This is one of the most useful irregular verbs. And this is why you need to learn its proper conjugation.

Subject	*AVERE*	Examples
(Io)	**ho**	*Ho i doni.* (I have the gifts.)
(Tu)	**hai**	*Hai noi.* (You have us.)
(lui/Lei)	**ha**	*Ha le riposte.* (He/She has the answers.)
(Noi)	**abbiamo**	*Abbiamo famiglia.* (We have family.)
(Voi)	**avete**	*Lo avete.* (You all have it.)
(Loro)	**hanno**	*Essi hanno l'un l'altro.* (They have each other.)

There are more verbs to learn. Keep reading Italian materials to expand your vocabulary.

Chapter 9 – TRAVEL VOCABULARY

Treat this chapter as your mini survival guide when traveling to Italy.

Finding Accommodation

Listed in this section are some of the most useful phrases you need to learn so you can converse with hotel staff and arrange your accommodation properly. Take your time in learning them.

Since you're new in the area, you may want to ask for recommendations. You can start with this.

Mi può consigliare...   meaning   Can you recommend...

...un albergo nel centro città?   meaning

...a hotel in the city centre?

...un albergo tranquillo?   meaning

...a quiet hotel?

...un albergo per famiglie?   meaning

...a family-friendly hotel?

...un albergo non costoso?   meaning

...an inexpensive hotel?

...un buon albergo?   meaning

...a good hotel?

Once at the hotel, you would want to find out if they still have rooms available so you start with this.

Ha una camera libera? meaning

Do you have a room available?

No, siamo al completo. meaning

No, we are booked out.

No, non abbiamo nessuna camera libera. meaning

No, we have no rooms available.

Sì, abbiamo ancora una camera libera. meaning

Yes, we still have rooms available.

Per quante persone? meaning

For how many people?

Per _____ persone. meaning

For ____ people

Per quante notti? meaning   For how many nights?

Per _____ notte meaning   For _____ night

Una camera singola o doppia? meaning

A single room or double room?

Quanto costa una camera _____ per _____ notti?

How much is it for a ___ room for _____ nights?

Una camera _____ costa _____ Euro per notte.

A _____ room costs _____ euros per night.

At the hotel, be mindful about these keywords so you can easily ask the hotel staff in case you need anything.

La chiave	meaning	The key
Quarto piano	meaning	Fourth floor
Terzo piano	meaning	Third floor
Secondo piano	meaning	Second floor
Primo piano	meaning	First floor
Piano terra	meaning	Ground floor
Rotto/rotta	meaning	Broken
La luce	meaning	The light
L'acqua	meaning	The water
Caldo	meaning	Hot
Freddo	meaning	Cold
Pulito	meaning	Clean
Rumoroso	meaning	Noisy
Sporco	meaning	Dirty

Il riscaldamento   meaning   The heater

l'aria condizionata meaning   The air conditioning

Food

Food is essential. The Italians are known for having a healthy appetite. Do not miss out and learn a few things about food or at least how to say them properly.

Il cibo	meaning	Food
Il panino	meaning	Sandwich
La bistecca	meaning	Steak
Le verdure	meaning	Vegetables
La frutta	meaning	Fruit
La salsiccia	meaning	Sausage
L'insalata	meaning	Salad
Il latte	meaning	Milk
L'uovo	meaning	Egg
Il formaggio	meaning	Cheese
La torta	meaning	Cake
Il burro	meaning	Butter
Il pane	meaning	Bread

At the restaurant, you may encounter these words. Here are a few questions you should expect and the right way to answer them.

Cosa desidera ordinare? meaning Would you like to order?

Non lo so ancora. meaning I don't know yet.

Un momento per favore. meaning One moment, please.

Cosa mi può raccomandare? meaning What can you recommend?

If you know what to order you can start with *Io vorrei...* (I would like...) or *Io prendo...* (I will have...)

As you look through the menu, you will most likely encounter these terms.

L'antipasto	meaning	Appetizer or Starter
Il primo	meaning	First Course
Il secondo	meaning	Entree / Main Course
Il manzo	meaning	Beef
Il pollo	meaning	Chicken
Il maiale	meaning	Pork
La pasta	meaning	Pasta
La carne	meaning	Meat
Il riso	meaning	Rice
Le patate	meaning	Potatoes
La zuppa	meaning	Soup

Il contorno	meaning	Side Dish
Il dolce	meaning	Dessert
Lo Champagne	meaning	Champagne
Lo spumante	meaning	Bubbly or Champers
Il vino bianco	meaning	White wine
Il vino rosso	meaning	Red wine
La birra	meaning	Beer
Il succo di frutta	meaning	Juice
L'acqua minerale	meaning	Mineral Water

Finally, this is not something you would see on the menu but you would want to familiarize yourself with, *la mancia* (tip).

Conclusion

Congratulations!

You are now one language smarter than when you started!

You see, it wasn't that bad. In fact, you should be proud of yourself. You may still have a long way to go but you're off to a great start. Continue practicing what you learned and pile up more Italian words to your vocabulary.

Finally, if you enjoyed this book, please take the time to share your thoughts and post a positive review on Amazon. It'd be greatly appreciated!

Thank you and good luck!